Breaking Through

21-Day Devotional for Reigniting Dreams and Living the Life God Created You to Live

Joshua Olmos

Copyright 2019 by Joshua Olmos

All rights reserved. No part of this publication may be reproduced, distributed or transmitted in any form or by any means, including photocopying, recording, or other electronic or mechanical methods, without the prior written permission of the publisher, except in the case of brief quotations embodied in critical reviews and certain other noncommercial uses permitted by copyright law.

Although the author and publisher have made every effort to ensure that the information in this book was correct at press time, the author and publisher do not assume and hereby disclaim any liability to any party for any loss, damage, or disruption caused by errors or omissions, whether such errors or omissions result from negligence, accident, or any other cause.

Adherence to all applicable laws and regulations, including international, federal, state and local governing professional licensing, business practices, advertising, and all other aspects of doing business in the US, Canada or any other jurisdiction is the sole responsibility of the reader and consumer.

Neither the author nor the publisher assumes any responsibility or liability whatsoever on behalf of the consumer or reader of this material. Any per-ceived slight of any individual or organization is purely unintentional.

The resources in this book are provided for informational purposes only and should not be used to replace the specialized training and professional judgment of a health care or mental health care professional.

Neither the author nor the publisher can be held responsible for the use of the information provided within this book. Please always consult a trained professional before making any decision regarding treatment of yourself or others.

ISBN: 978-0-578-53422-0

"Our greatest fear should not be of failure, but of succeeding at something that doesn't really matter."

—D.L. Moody

Table of Contents

Intro 7

More to Life Than This 9
Can These Bones Live? 13
Sharpen Your Ax 21
Life Is in the Blood 27
Start 33
Be the First 39
Relationship 45
Trust God 51
Obedience Is Better Than Sacrifice 55
Day by Day 61
Stand for What's Right 67
Ambassador 73
Standard 79
Where Are You Getting Your Information? ... 85
Favor 91

Etch-a-sketch	95
Fear of Man or of God	99
Character vs. Reputation	105
The Past Doesn't Matter	109
Made to Create	113
Walk With the Wise	119
About the Author	125

Intro

My story didn't have the best of beginnings. I was abandoned when I was 13, left to be homeless. I joined a gang, went to jail, became an alcoholic, and much more. I'm sure if you think about it, you could probably also say that you didn't have the best of beginnings. The great thing about being a Christian is that this isn't how our story ends.

My testimony isn't only about the hard places the Lord has taken me out of. It's also about what He did inside of me. I no longer feel like that frightened, unloved, anxious, and depressed kid from the beginning of that story. The Bible says you're a new creation, old things have passed away and you've become new **(2 Corinthians 5:17)**. Believe this because it's true. We don't have to live in the past or with old hurts. They can be wiped away and forgotten. Today can be the start of your new life, and you can cancel your subscription to past issues now. Isaiah 43 says to not dwell on the past because God is doing a new thing in you. How amazing is that? We can have a breakthrough in our lives, even from past hurts!

You may be saying, "This sounds great, but how in the world do I do that?" Trust me; I understand what it's like to struggle with overwhelming feelings and seemingly insurmountable roadblocks, not knowing how to move forward in the life I knew I was supposed to live. That's why I wrote this book, to help people like you. In this book, you find biblical principles that will help get you from where you are now to living the life you were created to live.

More to Life Than This

At one point in my early twenties, I felt as though I had seen what life had to offer, and it was far from satisfying. On the outside, life was business as usual, hanging out with friends, family, and working. But on the inside, rang the sound of quiet desperation. I was desperately looking for some glint of hope that would save me from this "normal" life. There had to be more to life than this; there just had to be.

I've found this is often the truth for many people. Life, in itself, is just unsatisfying. The reason for this is that you were made for more than just living a normal, quiet life. You were made to be a world changer, an heir to the greatest King who has ever lived. You were planned before the foundation of the earth to do amazing things.

Something deep inside you knows this to be true. So why the disconnect? What's keeping you from doing what you know you were made to do? The answer is one I never expected. Surrender. When we surrender to the One who made us, to the One who knows us better than we know ourselves, when we surrender to the One who loves us more than anyone we know, then we can line up with how we were meant to live.

The Bible says our ways aren't God's ways **(Isaiah 55:8)**. This means we can't do what we were born to do our own way but must surrender ourselves to the One who knows best. Once we do that, the impossible becomes possible, the cloudy become clear and that frustration becomes hope. You see a light at the end of the tunnel, but you can't dig yourself out. Let the One who built the tunnel show you the way.

If something in your life isn't lining up to how the Bible says it should, then check and see if you're surrendering that part of your life to Jesus? Once His Word becomes greater than your thoughts on the matter, things start becoming clearer. If your whole life seems to be on repeat, it's time to surrender to Jesus Christ and begin the relationship that will change your life forever.

Whichever one of these situations you're in, you can turn it around right now. All you have to do is talk to God, surrender your life, and let Him direct your path from now on.

Time to Reflect

*What parts of your life have you not fully surrendered to God?

prayer life

Free Time

Isaiah 55:8

My thoughts are not your thoughts, neither are my your ways my ways declares the Lord.

When these things pop up again, remind yourself out loud that you're surrendering these things to God.

Can These Bones Live?

Oftentimes, we can look at our lives and think, "How did I get here? This isn't how it was supposed to be; this isn't how life was supposed to turn out." We had hopes and dreams and plans. Somewhere along the way, life got away from us and what we thought was supposed to happen didn't pan out.

This is what happened to the nation of Israel. God had promised them something. They hoped and dreamed of it coming to pass, but when they looked around, it seemed impossible. They were torn from their homeland. They were beaten and broken, living among their enemies. How had God's chosen people ended up like this? How have you, a child of God, ended up like this?

In **Ezekiel 37**, God took the prophet Ezekiel to the valley of dry bones and asked him a question. The valley of dry bones was a symbol of the nation of Israel, the people who were once thought to be the mightiest nation but now lay waste in the desert forgotten. "Son of man, can these bones live?"

(Ezekiel 37:3a). Look out at your life and what it was supposed to be and ask yourself the same question, "Can this dream live?" Oh, how we hope to say yes, but much like Ezekiel looking out over those dry bones in the desert, we can't see how they could. Ezekiel's answer was one of great wisdom. He said, "Only you know, Lord" **(Ezekiel 37:3b)**.

The Lord then instructed Ezekiel to prophesy to the bones, "Prophesy to these bones and say to them, 'Dry bones, hear the word of the Lord! This is what the Sovereign Lord says to these bones: I will make breath enter you, and you'll come to life. I will attach tendons to you and make flesh come upon you and cover you with skin; I will put breath in you, and you'll come to life. Then you'll know that I am the Lord.'" So I prophesied as I was commanded. And as I was prophesying, there was a noise, a rattling sound, and the bones came together, bone to bone. I looked, and tendons and flesh appeared on them and skin covered them, but there was no breath in them. Then he said to me, "Prophecy to the breath; prophesy, son of man, and say to it, 'This is what the Sovereign Lord says: Come, breath, from the four winds and breathe into these slain, that they may live.'" So I prophesied as he commanded me, and breath entered them; they came to life and stood up on their feet—a vast army. Then he said to me: "Son of man, these bones are the people of Israel. They say, 'Our bones are dried up and our hope is gone; we're cut off.' Therefore prophesy and say to them: 'This is what the Sovereign Lord says: My people, I'm going to open your graves and bring you up from them; I will bring you back to the land of Israel. Then you, my people, will know that I am the Lord when I open your graves and bring you up from them. I will put my Spirit in you and you'll live, and I will settle you in your own land. Then you'll know that I the Lord have spoken, and I have done it, declares the Lord'" **(Ezekiel 37: 4-14)**.

When you look at your life and it seems to have passed you by and hope has been lost, it's not up to you to figure out how to get it back on track. If you knew how to do that, you would have done it already. You must go to God and say, "Only you know, Lord, how to fix this," and wait for Him to tell us what to do. For he's the one who knows how to bring dead things back to life and restores that which was once thought lost to its rightful place.

It doesn't matter what we have done or what our past looks like. All things can be restored, and all things can be new. The Bible says He makes all things new and we're a new creation in Christ Jesus. Don't let anything in your past hold you back.

You may be asking yourself, "Well, if He *can* do it, why doesn't He just *do it*?" When God told Ezekiel to prophesy to the bones, do you think the bones didn't hear Him as well? If I were to ask you to ask the person next to you to hand me something, do you think they would wait for you to hand it to me? Or do you think they would give it to me once they heard me ask for it? Most likely it would be the latter, but bones only moved when Ezekiel told them to, and this is because God has made us co-laborers with Him. He wants to work through us and not just bypass us to do what He wants. He has given us the power of life and death in our mouth. He can fix your situation for you and just set you in it, but He loves to work with you to do the impossible.

Bringing things we once thought were dead back to life takes us looking to God for instructions and not trying to fix things on our own. If self could help, it would. No matter what it looks like or how long those dreams have been dead, He will show you how to make the impossible possible. He knows the plans He has for you, and they're plans to prosper you and not to harm you **(Jeremiah 29:11)**. You know you were made for greater things than this; you know there's more to life than what you see right now. Don't let the world trick you into believing it's too late or that it can't be done. With God all things are possible **(Matthew 19:26)**.

Hebrews 11:6 says in order to come to God, you must believe that He is and that He's a rewarder of those who seek Him. You need to let yourself believe this again. You must let yourself hope and trust God like you did when you were first saved.

Time to Reflect

*What dreams have you let die?

Believe these dreams can still happen and trust God will show you what He wants you to do.

Sharpen Your Ax

Years ago, I had a conversation with my father-in-law that I'll never forget. My wife and I were newly married, and we had just moved into a two-bedroom apartment. I had a newborn and a two-year-old at the time. We weren't doing well financially and, even though I was working two jobs and my wife was working one, we still weren't making enough money. We were upside down every month. The bills were piling up.

One night, while visiting my in-laws, my father-in-law started asking me about our finances and how things were going. My father-in-law, who is a brilliant businessman, could see right through our "everything is fine" facade. He knew the numbers weren't adding up and we had to be drowning in debt.

That night, we had a good conversation, and my in-laws were great, but there was one thing above all else I took away from that night. I asked him what I needed to know to never be in that situation again.

Even if my debt were erased in one night, I wouldn't know how to keep myself out of debt because I still wasn't earning enough to break even every month. I didn't know how to build wealth, but only spent money trying to survive. How did I get from where I was to where he was? He didn't really have a specific answer for me, but something sparked in me that day.

The Bible says people perish for lack of knowledge **(Hosea 4:6, Proverbs 5:23)** and that was my story. I was dying because I didn't know how to get from point A to point B. From that night on, I was determined to learn everything I could about how to become the man I wanted to be. I read books on leadership, parenting, business, finances, and anything else I thought I needed. I was determined not to let my circumstances rob my family and me of a good life.

I wish I could say everything turned around after that, but it didn't. Books are great, and I believe in reading, a lot, but you need something more than just information. You need to know how and when to apply it. When I was young, someone told me there was a difference between knowledge and wisdom. I didn't completely understand what they meant until that moment when I realized all the information in the world did me no good if I didn't know how it applied to my real-life situation.

The Bible says in **Isaiah 1:17**, "Learn to do good." **Hebrews 5:14** says, "Solid food is for the mature, who because of practice have their senses trained to discern good and evil." I soon found that being led by the Holy Spirit is the only way to turn that information into real-life change. I had to learn how to hear His voice and understand when He was nudging me in a particular direction.

I'm happy to say, through my relationship with God and a little discipline, my family and I are now doing great. Prayer does work, and we're blessed because the Lord has kept us. It was because of that night's realization that I stopped trying to cut the trees with a dull ax and found how to sharpen my ax so I could clear a path. There's a solution to every problem and hope for every future. The hard part is that, sometimes, it isn't clear where to look for those answers. You don't understand what you don't understand. I wish someone would have come alongside me to help me figure things out. Life isn't always easy, but with God and your brothers and sisters in Christ, you don't have to do it alone.

Time to Reflect

*What are some things in your life you would like to learn? Ask yourself where the holes in your life are.

Jesus - all things Jesus
His ways, the way He loved
i was kind yet had boundaries
His bravery, His love for
us humans.

_____
_____
_____
_____
_____
_____
_____
_____
_____
_____
_____
_____
_____
_____
_____

Remember that with the guidance of the Holy Spirit and a little practice, you can make sure your ax is always sharp.

Life Is in the Blood

One day, while I was having coffee with my mentor, we were talking about how the Bible spoke of things before they were scientifically proven. One of those things is in **Leviticus 17:11**, where it says the life of the flesh is in the blood.

He mentioned how popular it was to have all these DNA tests now to know your family tree and know how you're connected to other people. Then he brought up a fascinating point. He said every cell knows its purpose and where it fits in the body. A heart cell knows it's a heart cell and a liver cell knows it's a liver cell. The ones that don't know where they belong are the ones that harm the body.

I pondered this for a while and realized how that was true not only in our bodies but also in the body of Christ. After I did a little research, I found that one of the many things that makes cancer cells different from normal cells is that when healthy cells hear the signal to stop growing, they do. Cancer cells don't pay attention to the signals given to them. In the body of Christ, those who cannot hear the voice of God for themselves end up hurting the body instead of helping it.

Another thing blood does is when the body gets injured, the cells around it help. Some help to cover it so nothing else gets in, while other cells patch up the wound. White blood cells are called in as well. So the body works together to help heal the injury, and when their job is done they go back to what they were doing before.

All of this fascinated me and made me realize how in control of everything the Lord is. He created our bodies to heal themselves and also told us how we're to help each other. He knows what each person is supposed to do and what we need in order to do it. You aren't alone. God not only put people in your path to help but also gave you all the tools you need to succeed.

There's more to this life than you may realize. There's more to you than you realize. Listen to that still, small voice inside of you and let Him direct your steps. He wants to talk with you. Read your Bible. He didn't make the Bible for Himself; He made it for you.

Read your Bible as if your Heavenly Father is trying to communicate with you because He is. The Bible isn't just some stories in a book. It's God's love story to you. He shares His heart and all about Himself in it. When you read it as though God is telling you about Himself and His relationship with you, you'll begin to see things He's been trying to say to you.

No matter what's going on in your life, know that you're loved. Cast your cares on Him because He cares for you **(1 Peter 5:7)**

Time to Reflect

*Go read the Bible and write down what the Lord shows you that you didn't realize before.

Forgiveness
Bitterness
Taking things that are said about others it doesn't reflect me in anyway shape or form.

Always remember that Jesus loves you and wants to have a real relationship with you.

Start

I believe in working smarter, not harder. I like to think and find out the best way to do something rather than just winging it. This seems very logical to me but I've realized that people who keep moving in the right direction seem to get more done than I do. For example, fitness is something I've struggled with for a long time. I go through phases when I become dedicated to getting back in shape. I clean up my eating and stick to a rigorous workout plan but then in a couple of months, I feel like I look good enough to slow down. Then I end up stopping and have to repeat the cycle every year. I have a friend who doesn't eat as well as he should and only does a minimal workout every day, but he's very fit. I know there are so many holes in his fitness structure because I've done so much research about what's best and what's not, but I don't have the sustained results he does.

I've learned that you cannot wait until everything is right or you have it all figured out to start. It takes a person moving forward when they don't think they have it all together before they start. You have to mentally toughen up and get moving if you want to accomplish anything in this life. I've hit a time in my life when I need to toughen up and keep working hard in every area in my life. When my son was just born, I realized how much I could get done and how much sleep I needed in a week. It hit me so hard when I noticed that I could have been living on this schedule and have gotten so much more accomplished.

I look at the people in my life whom I admire, and they're all very dedicated, hard-working people. It's time to become one of those people. It's time to stop making excuses and begin to start walking toward the things the Lord has told me to do.

It's better to take steps in the right direction and start moving toward the goal. Otherwise, we don't get anything done because we're trying to make sure everything is perfect before we do.

With the technology we have today, there's nothing we cannot look up and learn how to do. When you get stuck, pray and ask God for wisdom. **James 1:5** says, "But if any of you lacks wisdom, let him ask of God, who gives to all generously and without reproach, and it will be given to him." Many times, the issue isn't that we don't know what to do but that we won't get up and do it. Procrastination is a huge problem in our society. You'll be surprised by how much different your life looks when you stop trying to research everything and start walking out what you know to do.

The Bible talks about many things we should be doing, and the only reason many of us aren't doing them is because they're hard. The Bible says we shouldn't be in debt **(Proverbs 22:7 and 6:1-7)**, but it's hard only to use the cash you have and not get what you want when you want it. The Bible says that our body is a temple and we should take care of it **(1 Cor 6:19-20)** but we eat junk food and don't sleep as we should. There are many more examples like taking care of our things and reading the Word, but I think you get the point.

Sometimes, we wonder why God hasn't given us the next step when we haven't done the first things He has told us to do. That can all change today. Today, we can start walking toward the life God created us to have.

Time to Reflect

*What are some things in your life you know you need to start doing?

Morning Time w/ the Lord
going to bed earlier

_____

_____

_____

_____

_____

_____

_____

_____

_____

_____

_____

_____

_____

_____

_____

Remember that a righteous man may fall but they always get back up **(Proverbs 24:16)**. It may not be easy, but it will be worth it.

Be the First

Now that you know your dreams aren't dead and you can see yourself living the life you were meant to live, I want you to look at the examples the Bible gives us of living that life. As you read the Word of God, you'll notice example after example of people being the first of their kind to do something; Abraham, Joseph, Moses, David, Jesus, and Paul are just the names everyone recognizes. There are so many other people and stories of being the first in the Bible.

The Bible says to be imitators of Christ. It's easy to see how Christ was an example of going out and being the first at something, but He gave us many examples of others being the first. I believe this was done intentionally so you would know that what you've been called to do may have never been done before and that's okay. You're in good company.

The Bible says we can nullify the Word of God by our traditions **(Mark 7:13)**. Imagine if Abraham would have carried on the traditions of his people. He never would have been the father of faith, and the same goes for every other person I mentioned before. They never would have become who we know today. I'm not saying to rebel against your traditions for no reason, but I'm saying to never let anything nullify the Word of God. If God said it and it's in the Bible, it's right and don't let anyone ever convince you otherwise.

You can do all things through Christ who strengthens you **(Philippians 4:13)**. Just because no one else has done it before doesn't mean you can't be the first. Look around you. Everything you have and are using was first made by someone. Someone thought up the phone you use, the TV you watch, the car you drive, and so on. Imagine if they allowed someone to convince them they couldn't do that. What if you're meant to write something never written or make something no one made before. We thank God for our founding fathers, for Martin Luther King, for Billy Graham and many more who were the first of their kind to take a stand for what they believed in. What has been put in your heart? What can't you seem to shake no matter how hard you try?

There's nothing too small or too big. God knew you before the foundation of the world and knew you needed to be here now. If this world didn't need you,

you'd be home in Heaven with your father and not here behind enemy lines. Sometimes, it can be frustrating because it seems that no one really understands. There's a reason for that. You weren't made to be a copy but a pioneer. God knows why He created you and what you're meant to do. Go to God and ask Him.

Time to Reflect

*What's something you've always felt in your heart needed to be done, but nobody else seems to see?

_____

_____

_____

_____

_____

_____

_____

_____

_____

_____

_____

_____

_____

_____

Remember that you're not like anyone else and that's by design, not by accident.

Relationship

You may have noticed there's a common thread holding all these pages together: being able to talk to God and hear His voice. We must be able to listen to what God is saying to us in order to walk out our calling and what He would have us do. Hearing the voice of God and understanding the will of God in your life comes from the type of relationship you have with Him.

While I was reading about Moses in the Bible, I was amazed by how freely he and the Lord spoke to each other. In **Exodus 33:17**, God tells Moses, "I will also do this thing of which you have spoken; for you have found favor in My sight and I have known you by name." That's the type of communication and relationship I had hoped to have with God.

I want to find favor in His sight and have Him know me by name. That verse changed how I prayed and viewed my daily walk. I no longer was seeking that which I could get out of God but instead prayed about whether what I was doing was finding favor in His sight or not. Was I pleasing to God?

In **Matthew 7:21-23**, Jesus says, "Not everyone who says to Me, 'Lord, Lord,' will enter the kingdom of heaven, but he who does the will of My Father who is in heaven will enter. Many will say to Me on that day, 'Lord, Lord, did we not prophesy in Your name, and in Your name cast out demons, and in Your name perform many miracles?' And then I will declare to them, 'I never knew you; depart from Me, you who practice lawlessness.'"

How often have I gone about my day without giving a thought to the eternal weight of what I was doing? I've acted selfishly and given little thought to the thoughts and feelings of my Father in Heaven. Is this what the Lord meant when He spoke about forgetting your first love **(Revelation 2:4)**?

This, of course, made me stop and repent. My whole reason for being is to love the Lord and find favor in His sight. How often I prayed "Let your will be done," without really letting that sink in. But as I read this scripture, it did. I remembered my first love and, in doing so, was granted the gift of perspective. Things that seemed so important no longer mattered and things I had put to the side came back into focus.

It's a daily discipline to walk in a manner worthy of the Lord **(Colossians 1:10)**, but it has been worth it. Life once felt as though I was trying to survive it and, now, I couldn't imagine living life any other way. What a wonderful life it is when you get to walk it with the One who loves you more than anyone and knows what to do and say in every situation. To be able to see the hand of God in all you do and to be an extension of that hand to do the will of God here on earth is something that words do no service to. It must be experienced, not just spoken of.

The time is now, go and experience this life for yourself. He's just waiting to hear from you so you can begin that kind of relationship, too. No longer should we be seeking the hand of God for our own selfish ambitions. Rather, let us be seeking His face so that we would live holy (set apart) lives that fulfill His will here on earth.

The Bible says, "But seek first the kingdom of God and his righteousness, and all these things will be added to you **(Matthew 6:33)**." When our first priority is Him and not us, God makes sure we're completely taken care of.

Time to Reflect

*Are there parts of your relationship with God that could be better? What are they? What are you going to do to fix it?

_____

_____

_____

_____

_____

_____

_____

_____

_____

_____

_____

_____

_____

Remember that when you draw near to God, He will draw near to you **(James 4:8)**

Trust God

Like any healthy relationship, our walk with God must be birthed in trust. We must completely trust Him. Without that as our foundation, this walk, this life, will be challenging. It's very common to see Christians these days stress over little things and lose focus of the big picture. The Bible says in **1 Peter 5:7**, "Cast all your anxiety on him because he cares for you."

We can quickly get into a defensive mentality instead of an offensive mentality. We wait for the next thing to hit us instead of purposefully accomplishing what we were put here to do. We're not supposed to react to everything that comes our way but, instead, be purposeful about what we're doing and how we're living our life.

I said "mentality," not because I believe it's a new age thing, like "If we'll it to happen it will." Rather, I say it because the Bible says in **Romans 12:2** to "not be conformed to this world, but be transformed by the renewing of your mind, so that you may prove what the will of God is, that which is good and acceptable and perfect."

The Bible also says in **Matthew 11:28-30**, "Come to Me, all who are weary and heavy-laden, and I will give you rest. Take My yoke upon you and learn from Me, for I'm gentle and humble in heart, and you'll find rest for your souls. For My yoke is easy and My burden is light." If the yoke you're carrying isn't easy and the burden not light, could it be you're forgetting to leave your issues in God's hands?

This all stems from trusting God and what He says is true. If you don't trust Him, it's easy to try to take on the world by yourself and become overwhelmed. This is a defensive mentality, meaning you're always trying to resist attack. We're not called to survive the works of the enemy, but to destroy the works of the enemy **(1 John 3:8)**. When we fully trust God, we know He will take care of us as we walk out His will **(Philippians 4:19)**.

There's more to life than just trying to get by. The Bible says the fool puts his trust in himself **(Proverbs 28:26)**, but he who trusts in the Lord is blessed **(Psalm 84:12)**. It's time to renew our minds and start walking out and proving the good and acceptable will of God.

Time to Reflect

*Are you having trouble trusting God with things in your life? What does the Bible say about those things and trusting God?

_____

_____

_____

_____

_____

_____

_____

_____

_____

_____

_____

_____

Trust God • 53

Remember that God only wants the best for you and will never leave you or forsake you **(Hebrews 13:5)**

Obedience Is Better Than Sacrifice

Many Christians are striving to live a good Christian life. There are numerous interpretations of what that looks like. Whatever that looks like to you, you need to agree that it can't be done in your own strength or by your own method. You need the leading of the Holy Spirit and the guidance of the Word of God.

A funny meme says, "If you really want to know someone, make them use dial-up Internet." This is just a funny way of saying that you see the real side of a person when they're in a stressful situation. This is what we saw when King Saul was waiting for the prophet Samuel to arrive, and things weren't going well. In **1 Samuel 15**, King Saul ended up offering a sacrifice to God when it wasn't his place to do it. He thought he could get the ball rolling and make something happen even though he was told to wait. When Samuel arrived, he told King Saul that it was better to obey than to sacrifice. King Saul's response was to say that he did it because he feared the people and listened to them.

Word of advice, when God says you did something wrong just repent and don't make excuses. So what does this have to do with living a good Christian life? No matter what the circumstances are and no matter what's going on, always listen for the instruction of God. When things may seem to be going from bad to worse and there looks to be no way out, ask God what to do. The Bible says in all your ways acknowledge Him, and he will make your path straight. We can really make a mess of things when we try to do "good" without asking God what He wants to be done.

When God told Elijah to go find a widow because she would supply him with food in **1 Kings 17**, it seemed like a pretty straightforward word. When Elijah got there, however, the widow only had enough food for her and her son, she told Elijah that they were going to eat what they had left and die. Elijah could have very easily said, "Oh, well, don't worry about me. I can find food from someone else you seem like you have a lot going on." Instead, he obeyed the command of the Lord and said, "Well, before you do that, make me some food." If you know the story, you know a great miracle came from that act of obedience and the whole household was saved through it.

How hard would it have been for Elijah to sacrifice a meal or two in order not to bother this widow who was on her last leg? It wasn't about the food or Elijah; it was about accomplishing what the Lord wanted to be done in that town. It doesn't matter what it looks like; don't take it upon yourself to sacrifice something that was never meant to be sacrificed. Ask God what He wants to be done, and when He tells you, do it no matter what.

Living a life of obedience is a life lived in the will of God. Living a life of sacrifice without obedience is one lived in hardship. We're here to live out what God would have us accomplish, not to try to do our thing or live a life according to our own interpretation of what needs to happen.

Time to Reflect

*What things in your life have you sacrificed needlessly and will now let go of?

_____

_____

_____

_____

_____

_____

_____

_____

_____

_____

_____

_____

_____

Remember to acknowledge Him in all your ways and never do something just for the sake of doing it.

Day by Day

A pilot was making one of his usual routes when, all of a sudden, his instruments started going crazy, and the plane began to act erratically. He quickly radioed into dispatch and told them what was happening. The dispatcher had never heard of such a thing happening before, so he told the pilot to hold on. While he tried to figure out what was happening, a janitor, who was mopping a floor nearby, overheard the distress call and ran over to the dispatcher. He took the com from him and told the pilot, "I was a pilot in World War II Do exactly what I say, or that plane is coming down. Point the nose of the plane straight up and keep climbing until your instruments come back online. You have rats chewing through the wires." Sure enough, the pilot did as he was told and pretty soon his instruments came back online. When all was settled and the pilot was headed back to the terminal safely, the dispatcher asked the janitor why that had worked. The janitor informed him that we can survive at a higher altitude than the rats can, so climbing to a higher altitude would kill the rats.

When things in your life start to malfunction, and you can't seem to see your instrument panels very well, it may be that there are people or things chewing through your wires. Point the nose of the plane up so you can suffocate the rats and see things clearly again.

It can be easy to let the worries of this life get our attention more than the Lord. That still, small voice can be drowned out by all the things that claim to be important and must be handled now. There's nothing more important than hearing the voice of God for yourself. Often, we believe that living a good life here means taking care of all the day-to-day activities we have going on. We forget that the only day-to-day things we have in our lives should be that which facilitates what God would have us do. We're not to handle things first so we can spend time with God; God is life, and everything else should be accomplishing what God would have you do.

That sounds great, but I have a job and bills to pay and things to take care of, I can't just call in because I need to pray more. Well, you can, but I wouldn't advise it unless it's absolutely necessary. I would rather you get up earlier so you can spend time with Him before work and before life gets going. You'll find that when the Lord sets your schedule and not some outside pressure, your days run smoother and your time is better utilized. If you aren't being led by the Holy Spirit in all you do, life is going to be much harder than it was meant to be.

Jesus was the one person in this world who was pulled on more than anyone we know. Imagine knowing someone who can heal every sickness and disease, who can pull money out of fish, who commands the wind and the sea, and they obey. Everyone wanted time with Him and pulled on Him daily to hear their issues so He could fix it for them. When He spoke, thousands of people would go without eating so they wouldn't miss a single word. He would have to slip away from the crowds when He was done ministering to them, and when they realized He had gone, they would go looking for Him again.

Even with everyone pulling on Him, Jesus found time to pray to His father and was never shaken, confused, or overwhelmed by each day that came. He showed us how He did this. He never did it in His own power. Instead, He only did what His Father said to do and said what His Father said to say. This is a perfect example of how we're supposed to handle our lives. The problem is, we forget the power to overcome our day is in the ability to hear the Lord in every situation.

If you got into your car and tried to drive away but forgot the keys, you wouldn't get very far. Oh, sure, you could push your car or tow your vehicle. You could ride your bike or walk. But all of these would be harder than going back into the house and grabbing your keys. It's the same in your life. You can go throughout the day without praying, reading your Bible, and hearing the Lord's plan for the day, but it makes the day a lot harder than just getting up a little earlier and spending that quality time with God.

Time to Reflect

*What things are pulling on you and distracting you from spending time with God? What are you going to do when you feel them pulling on you?

_____
_____
_____
_____
_____
_____
_____
_____
_____
_____
_____
_____
_____

Remember to seek Him first and you'll be able to see everything else more clearly.

Stand for What's Right

When you get to know someone well enough, you can begin to see the patterns in their life. What type of food they like, what kind of things they're drawn to, their likes and dislike, etc. It's the same way with God. The more time we spend with Him, the more we see how He works and what pleases and displeases Him.

This knowing is what makes it easier to step out in faith. At times in our walk, we'll know that something needs to be said or done that goes against the status quo. We cannot shy away from these moments in our life. In the same way that God is jealous for us, we must be jealous for Him also. When Jesus saw the money changers in the temple, He knew that it displeased God, so something had to be done to make them stop. The Bible says to abhor what's evil and love what's good. I like that word "abhor." It means to not just hate something but also find it disgusting. When we see evil, it should disgust us. It should never be something that we ever get used to.

One day, while I was watching a movie about Winston Churchill, the Lord spoke to me. He told me I didn't hate evil like He hates evil. Then He had me turn to **Romans 12:9**. There, I saw what He was talking about. I didn't love sincerely if I allowed evil to hurt people and kept quiet because I didn't want to come across as unloving or judgmental. I need to hate evil and what it does to people the way the Lord does.

Our prayers shouldn't be filled with petitions for our needs but should be full of adoration and speaking that which is pleasing to God. Our lives must reflect this. You're here for a reason: not just to get by. but because there's something you have you have that this world needs. What does the Lord want to accomplish today through you? What can you do today that would be pleasing in His sight? The Bible says in **Ephesians 3:20**, "Now to Him who is able to do far more abundantly beyond all that we ask or think, according to the power that works within us." Are you allowing His power to work through you?

When your life reflects your love for God more than your needs, you'll find the evil in this world will want to attack you. When that happens, stand your ground, don't let up, and fight. When Paul was accused of doing evil when the man at the gate Beautiful was healed, he didn't back down. He stood his ground. What they called evil, he called good because it was good. Then in prayer, he asked for more boldness so he would continue the will of God.

Don't let anyone tell you what's right and what's wrong. Let the Bible and the Holy Spirit show you these things. The Bible says the Holy Spirit will lead you in all truth. Don't give the job of the Holy Spirit to a man. The closer we get to the return of Christ, the crazier this world gets. They don't know which way is up anymore and you would be foolish to follow this world. Spend time with God and in the Word so you may know His will and what He says is right and wrong. Pray that you may have the boldness to speak out against the evil in this world and what it's doing to people.

Time to Reflect

*What lies have you believed and will now take a stand against? What does the Bible say about them?

Remember that what the Bible says is wrong is wrong, no matter what this world says.

Ambassador

There are over 100 U.S. ambassadors right now. Ambassadors have many duties, but I want to focus on one of their benefits. Ambassadors have something called diplomatic immunity. Diplomatic immunity means they're exempt from most laws and taxes of the country they're in, but instead, abide by the rules set by their country.

The Bible says we're called to be ambassadors of Christ and, even though we're in this world, we're not of this world. Sometimes, I think we forget this about ourselves, that even though we live in this world, we're not called to abide by the rules of this world but of the Kingdom of God. Now that doesn't mean you don't pay your taxes and you rebel just for the sake of it. It does mean you're called to a life according to the Word of God and not one according to public opinion. The world's standards aren't our standards.

In the world of social media, it's easy to forget the Bible says the Holy Spirit will guide us in all truth and will teach us all things **(1 John 2:27)**. It's easy to hear so many opinions and voices of people who seem to have it all together and believe everything they say is true and right. In fact, our life and guidance come from the Kingdom of God and not from man.

That sounds great, but does it mean I shouldn't listen to anyone? No. It does mean you have to know what's man and what's God. When Jesus asked the disciples, "Who do you say that I am," Peter answered, "You are the son of God." Jesus then told Peter that no man had said that to him but that he had received that from God. What an amazing revelation. Then later, when Jesus told the disciples it was time for him to die on the cross, Peter said, "No, may it never be," and Jesus rebuked him and called him Satan. What happened? Both statements came from the same person. Why was one from God and one from Satan?

Not all things that come from a person are things you should trust. The Bible says to test the spirits, which means you have to know which spirit is speaking. Is it the anointing of God or the flesh or the devil using someone? The only way to know is to be connected to the Source. If you go by this world, it will all sound the same, and you may even be able to rationalize why something bad is good. It's not by our rationalization that we know the truth, but it's the Spirit of God that shows us the truth.

I want to touch on another part of being an ambassador. Ambassadors aren't allowed to share their own opinions on matters but must say what their countries wish them to say. As ambassadors of Christ, we must do the same. We can no longer speak our opinions on matters. We must say what the Bible says. The Bible says the power of life and death are in the tongue **(Proverbs 18:21)**. We must use our tongue for good and not for evil by speaking only that which the Lord would have us speak.

This also means we can no longer look at ourselves through the eyes of the world or believe everything people have said about us. We must only say about ourselves what the Bible says about us. We must only believe and speak what God speaks of us. The words that come from the Lord have the power to change not only the lives of others but our lives as well.

Time to Reflect

*What things are you going to stop speaking and replace with the words of God? Write down what the Word of God says about those things.

_____

_____

_____

_____

_____

_____

_____

_____

_____

_____

_____

_____

Remember that the power of life and death is in your tongue **(Proverbs 18:21)**

Standard

In 1954 an athlete named Roger Bannister did something no one thought was possible. He was the first person to run the mile in under 4 minutes. This was considered to be an impossible feat at the time. Since Roger broke that record 64 years ago, over 1400 people have gone on to do the same and even break Roger's record.

Isn't it amazing how many limitations in life are set because we don't believe they can be broken? Over 1,400 other people have run the mile in under 4 minutes. What was stopping people from doing it before Roger? It was only the belief that it couldn't be done.

How many areas of your life are you holding back in because you don't believe it can be done?

When did we stop believing we could do and live exactly the way the Bible says we can? When did the standard get lowered? When did the Word of God become suggestions and metaphorical ideas instead of an actual guide and command? We wonder why there's no power in our lives. We wonder why God doesn't seem to answer our prayers. We have become double-minded, holding unforgiveness and not fully surrendering. We expect to give Jesus half our heart and get a full cure. We're lovers of self and not lovers of God. We try to play the part of being a Christian without the relationship.

You can live a life that's just as anointed as Jesus's. The Bible says we can do even greater things than Jesus did, but for some reason, we don't believe it. We believe living life as a good Christian means abiding by the standards that have been set by other Christians. We have forgotten the standard that Jesus and the Bible say this life is intended to be walked out in. Oh, how different our lives could be if we let the Holy Spirit etch-a-sketch our thinking and the limits we have put on ourselves.

Jesus cursed a tree, and it withered and died. For some reason, we think that's just a metaphor for things in our life. We cannot ignore that the disciples saw the power of God in the natural and not just metaphorically. Jesus's works were both seen and heard.

When we remember that Jesus was a real person who became poor so we might become rich and that He who knew no sin became sin so we might be restored to God, it changes everything. We begin to live a life that's based on our relationship with Him and not one based on any human wisdom.

The Bible says He delights in the fear of the Lord and that the fear of the Lord is the beginning of all wisdom. Do you remember when you fell in love with your spouse? How no one could tell you any different, and you didn't care what people said or thought? You were in love and only that person's opinion mattered. The Bible says, "This I hold against you, that you have forgotten your first love **(Revelations 2:4)**." Have we forgotten that nothing else matters but God and doing what He says? We shouldn't care about the doctrine people have created to excuse why they're not living out the life Christ said we could have. It's time to reset and fall back in love with Jesus. It's time to live the life you were created to live and not the one you settled for.

Time to Reflect

*What areas of your life do you need to stop living by other people's standards and break through to what God has for you?

_____

_____

_____

_____

_____

_____

_____

_____

_____

_____

_____

Remember that you can do anything the Lord tells you to do, even if it has never been done before.

Where Are You Getting Your Information?

Today, I listened to a pastor speak on leadership and what it took to lead a church. This is a major church whose name I'm sure many would recognize. He has built an amazing organization that has done great things to advance that kingdom. I'm not going to mention his name because who he is doesn't matter but rather what I noticed while listening to him speak.

I noticed, halfway through the message, that he hadn't used one Bible verse or even referenced a Bible story. He was pulling on his own experience and things he had studied and learned along his journey. He had an amazing testimony and had learned a lot, but everything was being measured by his own experience or that of someone else.

This made me realize how common it is these days to speak from experience rather than from the Word of God. Don't get me wrong, I know that a testimony is a powerful thing and that we overcome the enemy by the Blood of the Lamb and the word of our testimony. The issue isn't the testimony; the issue is that our testimony should never be set as the standard. We should be modeling our lives after Christ and not another person.

I thought of all the leadership books I read and tried to remember how many of them were people's own findings and how many were straight from the Bible. This made me want to study the Bible and see what it said on leadership.

One thing I found was how Jesus was a very different kind of leader than I see now. For example, when Jesus was traveling, some people didn't like Him. Two of His disciples, James and John, wanted to call down fire from Heaven and destroy them. Now, if they were on our staff, they probably would have been let go. Wanting to commit murder is perhaps not a quality we would want in our ministers. We would have at least given them anger management classes or something, right? What did Jesus do? He rebuked them but didn't take away their power and, in fact, had them go out without Him into different cities, preaching the Gospel. I'm not sure we would allow those two to represent us so quickly after pulling a stunt like that.

I'm not writing this to teach on what I found the Bible said on leadership, even though there are many interesting things on that topic. I'm writing this is to ask you where you get your examples and instructions from. Is the Bible and Holy Spirit your guide or are you taking peoples word for how things ought to be? It shocked me how many times I've taken the word of someone without looking to see if scripture backed it up. It has become commonplace of Christians to be imitators of man and not of Christ.

Time to Reflect

*What are some things you're going to go back and check to see what that Bible says about it? Write what you find about it in the Bible here.

_____

_____

_____

_____

_____

_____

_____

_____

_____

_____

_____

_____

Remember that we must always get our information from the source and not from people's opinion.

Favor

When we pray for the favor of God to be on our lives, I wonder if we truly understand what that means. In the first chapter of Luke, an angel of the Lord appears to Mary and tells her that she's highly favored of the Lord. He then tells her she will give birth to Jesus, who will save the whole world. Wow, what an amazing word to get. I'm sure this is something most of us would love to hear: that we're highly favored of the Lord and we're going to be a part of something that's going to change the world forever.

The part in this story we often forget is that because of the favor of the Lord, Mary was put in a position that brought ridicule and finger-pointing and led to Mary being an outcast in her community. When God favors us, and our lives line up with His will, it usually means this world is going to hate us. In fact, that's exactly what Jesus told the disciples. The world is going to hate you.

How often we forget that. Walking out the will of God in your life may not always be easy, and many people may not understand. When I first surrendered my life to God, like actually surrendered everything, God told me I had to move away from everyone I knew to a place He would show me. This brought an onslaught of criticism. Friends, family, and people I didn't even know were telling me I was doing the wrong thing. They tried to reason with me, quote scripture to me, and scold me. To be honest, if I had seen a 24-year-old with two little kids, wife gone in the military, and no money, I would have probably thought it foolish for him to go on his own and leave everything behind also. But I had heard from God and was going to do what He said.

When you hear from God, you must make the same choice, no matter what people think or say. You must have a determination to fulfill the word of the Lord no matter what or who comes against you. It would be much easier to live a life with no persecution and no hardship. The Lord didn't say we would have an easy life but that He would give us the strength to endure anything that may come our way. God's word will come to pass just the way He said it would. Don't give up. Don't grow weary in well doing because, in due season, you'll reap the reward. **(Galatians 6:9)**

Time to Reflect

*What's something in your life God has told you about that you're not going to let anyone move you on?

Staying faithful to the things that the Lord has placed in my life

Remember that you can do all things through Christ who strengthens you **(Philippians 4:13)**

Etch-a-sketch

I've had a few management jobs in my time. In those jobs, a saying was passed around to the new managers in my division: "It's easier to teach someone new to do something right than it was to try to break bad habits." This was a spin on, "It's hard to teach an old dog new tricks."

I've come to realize this is true not only in management but also in every area of life, especially our walk with Christ. At one point in my life, I just seemed to be having a hard time breaking through to the next level in my relationship with God. I was doing what I thought I was supposed to do, yet I just felt like I was in a rut. One night while praying, I asked the Lord what was going on. I prayed in that vein for a while and didn't feel like I got an answer. The next morning, I woke up and went to grab a cup of coffee when, all of a sudden, I felt the Lord say to me that I had allowed myself to be deceived.

I didn't truly understand what that meant, but I wanted to find out, so I grabbed my coffee and prayed. In that prayer time, the Lord took me and, like an etch-a-sketch, erased everything I thought I knew. That's when it became clear. I had listened to other people's voices more than God's. I had let other people guide my life more than God guided me. **Mark 7:13** came to me. It says that we nullify the Word of God because of our traditions. I had taken what others had said as truth rather than looking to the Holy Spirit and Bible myself to see if it was as they said.

I had become stuck in my ways, not willing to go back and learn the right way. I was trying to make Christianity fit into my beliefs rather than changing my life to line up with the Word of God. So many people have used their life experiences as the measure for truth when the Bible says let God be found true and every human a liar. We are not to follow human standards. We're to obey God.

Don't fall into the trap I found myself in. Be willing to humble yourself and relearn how to live this life the right way. It doesn't matter who taught you what. It doesn't matter how long you've been doing something. Surrender it all to Christ and do what He says, even if it seems like you're the only one doing it that way.

Time to Reflect

*Plan out a time and write it down here to ask God to show you anything you need to relearn.

_____

_____

_____

_____

_____

_____

_____

_____

_____

_____

_____

_____

_____

Remember that when you humble yourself in the sight of the Lord, He will lift you up **(James 4:10)**.

Fear of Man or of God

Sometimes we can look at Bible stories and think, "How could people do that," or, "Why didn't they see that coming?" It's easy to cast judgment when we're looking from the outside in and not realize we may be doing the exact same thing they're doing.

This was my story not too long ago. I was reading the Bible story about David and Goliath. Each time I read it, I think to myself, *Why, out of all the people there, was David the only one to stand up to Goliath?* I found myself judging them a little bit for not being bolder and standing up for God. I found myself thinking things like, *Goliath is only a man, don't you know God is greater?* I considered them cowards for not standing up to Goliath.

Then it hit me. Every time I value someone else's opinion over God's or believe something can or can't be done because of what I see or hear, I'm doing the same thing. It was easy for me to fear man more than to fear God because I was relying on my senses to tell me what was true. I wasn't relying on the

Word of God and the Holy Spirit to tell me what was right. I had done this over and over in my life and hadn't even realized it.

I had even gone so far as to value the opinion of other ministers over what the Word of God said. Remember, Paul said that the Bereans were nobler than most because they searched the scriptures daily to see if what was being said was true. How many times had I just taken something as truth because it was preached in a sermon? How many times did I think things had to be a certain way because our culture said it was so? How many times was I afraid to speak out because I was afraid of what someone might say or think? All of that came from fearing man over God, and I realized my priorities had been out of sorts.

We're not supposed to go by what we see and hear but by the Word of God **(Isaiah 11:3)**. Now, this is easier said than done. I'm sure you can think of many times in your life when what you saw or heard made you wonder if what you knew to be right was even possible. I know I have.

The good news was once I knew what was wrong, it wasn't hard to fix. The first thing I did was repent for my ways and thoughts. Next, I had to figure out how to reset myself and line up with the will of God. For me, that was a matter of remembering all that Jesus had done for me on the cross. How amazing it was that our Father God would send His Son to earth to bear our sins. That we may be restored to Him and once again have a relationship with Him. Then in Joshua, it says to keep the books of law on your lips continually and to meditate on the Word. So I started reading and quoting scripture all day long. That way, I couldn't think about what other people thought or said because I was too busy reading and speaking scripture.

The added benefit to reading and quoting scripture all day was that now I knew what the Bible said about things. I could measure anything that came at me against the Word of God, which, in turn, increased my faith. This gave me boldness to speak out when the Lord told me to.

It would be an understatement to say this changed my life. I had no idea how the fear of man had hindered my relationship with God and had made my walk so much harder and stress-filled than it was meant to be. It was like a weight I didn't even know was there had been lifted, and I could see clearly. Don't let any person dictate your relationship with God or what you believe to be true. The Bible says the Holy Spirit will guide you in all truth. Make sure your guide is the Bible and the Holy Spirit.

Time to Reflect

*What opinions have you been listening to more than God? What does God say about that?

Remember that when you submit everything to God, He will make your path straight **(Proverbs 3:6)**.

Character vs. Reputation

Something I've heard repeatedly throughout my ministry life is that the devil will try to destroy my reputation, so be careful with it. Though I do believe this to be true, I believe it's more important to concern myself with my character than my reputation.

Jesus said, "If they hate you, know that they hated me first." When Jesus had one of the biggest crowds in front of Him, He said you couldn't follow Him unless you drank His Blood and ate His flesh. He also said if you didn't hate everything in proportion to loving Him, you couldn't be his disciple. Now, this doesn't sound to me like someone who cared very much about what people thought of Him.

It's hard to control your reputation because it's what others think and say about you. With social media and everyone having an opinion about everything these days, you're not going to be able to please everyone. The Bible say for those who have ears, let them hear. Isn't that really why they wanted to kill

Jesus? They didn't have ears to hear the truth, so he had a bad reputation in the eyes of the synagogue leaders of His time. You can, however, control your character and make sure you walk in a manner worthy of your calling. If you walk uprightly before God, who cares what others think of you. In fact, the Bible talks about how the more you choose to walk according to God's will, the more the enemy will attack you. But don't be troubled by it because He will be with you.

Do what's right in the sight of the Lord and don't listen to what the general public has to say about it. There will always be online trolls, hecklers, media looking for a splash, and people who just don't understand what you're saying. Don't speak in your own wisdom. Speak only that which the Father tells you to speak and you'll be great. Great, not because this world will praise you, but because your Father in heaven will see you and reward you.

Time to Reflect

*What are some things you need to take a bolder stance on?

Remember to not grow weary in well doing because God will reward you for persevering **(Galatians 6:9)**.

The Past Doesn't Matter

Oftentimes, the only thing that's holding us back from walking the path we were created to walk is ourselves. We can hold ourselves back because we don't see ourselves through the eyes of Jesus but can only see the bad in us. It's natural for us to be harder on ourselves than other people, but we cannot let things we've done stop us from doing what God has called us to do.

My story didn't start out on the best foot, but my testimony isn't just about the places from which the Lord has delivered me. It's about what God did inside of me. That's your story, too. God doesn't only change our circumstances; He washes away our sins and makes us a new person.

Don't be the stumbling block in your own life. Don't believe the lie that you're not good enough or that your past disqualified you from living the life God has called you to. We don't have to live in the past or with past hurts. They can be wiped away and forgotten. When we repent, God is faithful and just to forgive us of our sins. We must also forgive ourselves of these sins. We shouldn't bring up what the Lord has forgotten. Moving forward, it's important to remember what God says about us, no matter what the past was. **2 Corinthians 5:17** says, "Therefore if anyone is in Christ, he's a new creature; the old things passed away; behold, new things have come."

Today can be the start of your new life, and you can cancel your subscription to old issues right now. **Isaiah 43** says to not dwell on the past because God is doing a new thing in you. How amazing is it that we can have a breakthrough in our life even from past hurts!

Time to Reflect

*What are some things from the past you need to let go of?

_____

_____

_____

_____

_____

_____

_____

_____

_____

_____

_____

_____

_____

_____

_____

_____

_____

_____

_____

_____

_____

_____

_____

_____

_____

_____

_____

_____

_____

_____

Remember that you're a new creation and old things have passed away **(2 Cor 5:17)**

Made to Create

I'm blessed to have a wife and three great boys. One night, while we were sitting and having a family movie night, I looked around and it struck me how different we all are. One of my most favorite things is to watch a funny movie with my wife because her laughter fills the room and brings joy to all who hear it. My oldest son is very logical and catches a lot of subtext and little details of a movie you wouldn't notice unless pointed out to you. My middle son is a photographer and he will see the beauty in almost anything. My youngest son is only three, but it's incredible to watch how much he takes in and processes. It amazes me how we all tackle and see things differently.

The Bible says God created us in His image, yet not one of us is the same. Not even two of us have the same fingerprints, and He has passed that creativity to us. There's a reason why, even though you may be similar to someone, you're not the same. Sometimes, that can make you feel lonely, but you must see the real reason it's this way.

You're made for a specific reason. It's not a mistake that you're here. No one can do what you can do. I'm not talking about someone taking your job. I'm talking about the very reason you were created, the reason God made you and knew you had to be here at this time. Imagine what life would be like without Henry Ford or Abraham Lincoln. The world would look different right now.

You may be thinking you can't do what they did. Well, that's true, because that's not why you're here. They already did what they were meant to do. What are you meant to do? What tugs at your heart, what needs to be addressed that's being overlooked? What needs to be made, what needs to be taught? Only you and God know the answer to those questions, but one thing is for certain: you have a purpose. The way you see things isn't an accident, and it didn't happen by chance.

You have the power of life and death in your tongue. You were made to create and change the world around you. You either line up with the will of God for your life, or you can live life always longing for more. When you don't walk in the will of God, there will always be something missing. The Bible shows us example after example of world changers. That wasn't done by accident, that was done for you. Your heavenly Father is showing you something. It's time to embrace who He made you to be. It's time to go out and live out the will of God for your life.

Time to Reflect

*What creative abilities did God give you that not everyone else has?

Remember that you're wonderfully made by God **(Psalm 139:14)**.

Walk With the Wise

There's only so much we can accomplish alone. We're made to connect with other people. The Bible says we're all different parts of one body.

The most crucial part is making sure you're connected with the right people. Being connected to the wrong people can be like connecting your leg to your head. Sometimes it's worse than not connecting with anyone at all. In **Proverbs 13:20**, the Bible says he who walks with the wise will be wise but if you walk with fools, harm will come to you.

You need to hang around the people from whom you can learn, those who have vision and can see beyond what's right in front of you. Not everyone will understand you and that's okay. Hang around the ones who do and don't worry about the ones who can't see what you see. They may just be a different part of the body.

Don't let people speak doubt around you. Don't let people try to bring you down. It's vital that you only allow people who speak faith and the Word of God into your life.

Only, walking with the wise may not always look the way we think it should either. Many times, we can be attracted to people who are "the best" in their field, but we must remember to look at more than just external qualifications. The Bible says in **Psalms 1:1** that we're blessed if we don't take counsel from the ungodly. It doesn't matter how good a person is in worldly things, we must not let anyone speak into our lives who doesn't know God for themselves.

I know this seems like a very bold statement and can be an even harder thing to do, but we must obey the standard the Lord has set before us. We'll be blessed if we do. Remember, we're not trying to be a copy of the world. We're accomplishing the plans and purposes of God. To do this, we must do it His way. That's the only way to do what has never been done before.

Many Godly people are gifted in areas you're not, and, together, you can accomplish so much. Don't let setbacks or past hurts keep you from connecting with your brothers and sisters in Christ. The enemy would like nothing more than to put a wedge between you and those you're supposed to walk with.

You may not always walk with them. It may only be for a season, but you must continue to learn and grow. You cannot let what you see or hear stop you from accomplishing what the Lord created you to do. You can do all things through Christ who strengthens you **(Philippians 4:13)**.

Time to Reflect

*Do you know wise people with whom you need to connect? Pray that God will show you the right way to do that and write it down.

Remember that wisdom is better than gold and silver.

About the Author

Joshua has been working in ministry since 2011. He has had the opportunity to partner with many on-fire ministries across the U.S. In 2018, he founded Olmos Ministries, a Christian outreach dedicated to developing faith in Jesus Christ and helping others fulfill the call they have on their life. His experiences have provided unique ministry opportunities at home and across the nation.

Joshua and his wife Stephanie live near Reno, NV, have been together since 2002, and have three beautiful children. When not ministering, he enjoys spending time out in nature, taking his family on hikes, exploring God's creation.

Need More Help?

If you need more information on anything that was covered in this book or prayer as you start on your journey to the life God has created you to live, please visit us at:

website: olmosministries.org

email: info@olmosministries.org

or send a letter to:
Olmos Ministries
PO Box 206
Sparks NV 89432.

Thank You For Reading My Book!

I really appreciate all of your feedback, and I love hearing what you have to say.

Please leave me an honest review on Amazon letting me know what you thought of the book.

Thanks so much!
Joshua Olmos

Made in the USA
Columbia, SC
28 August 2019